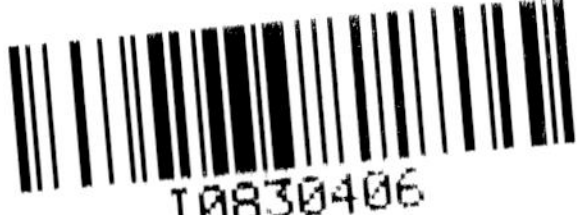

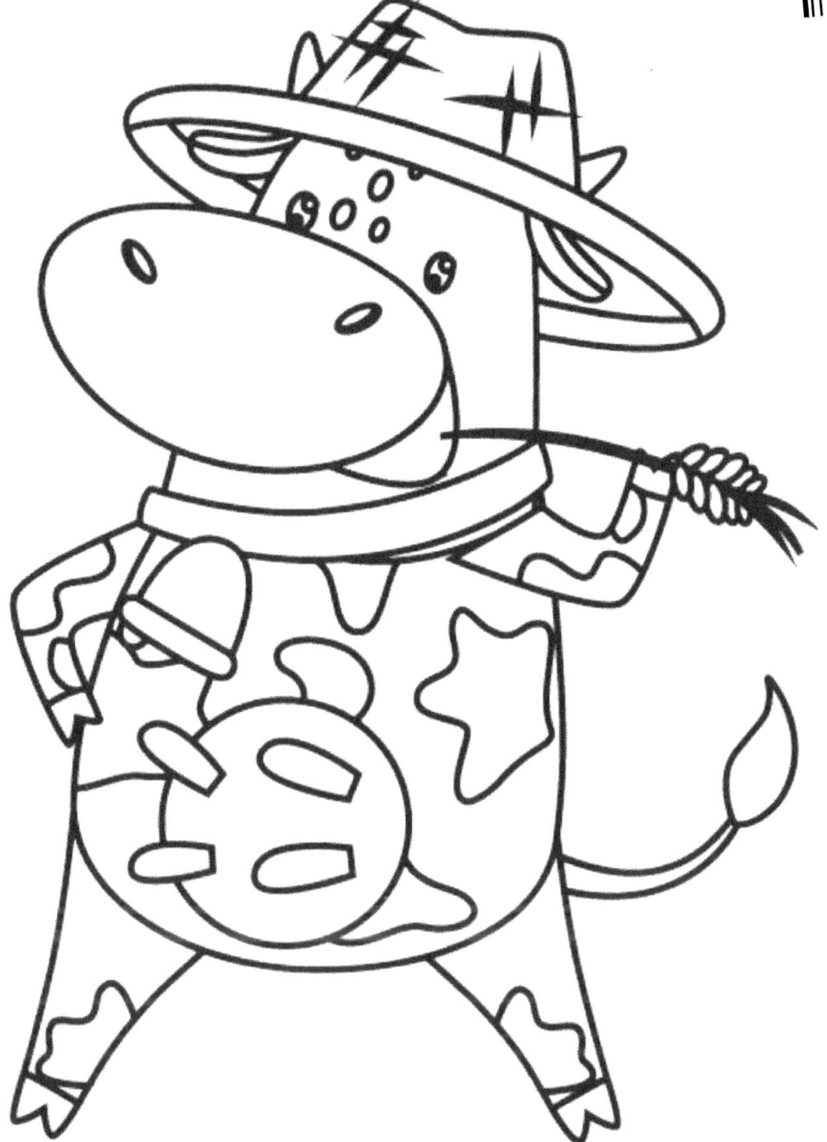

This Book Belongs To

COLOR TEST

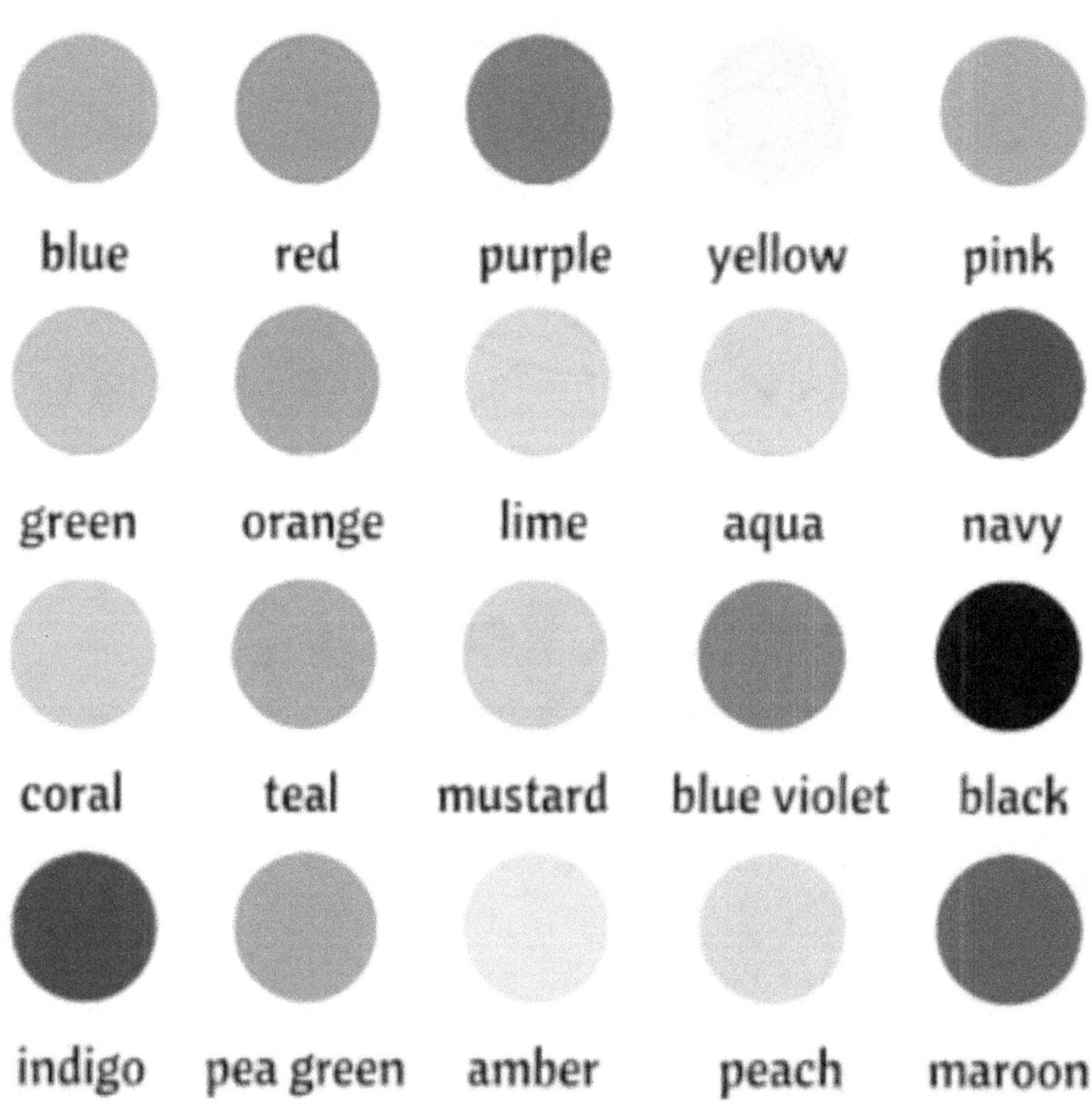

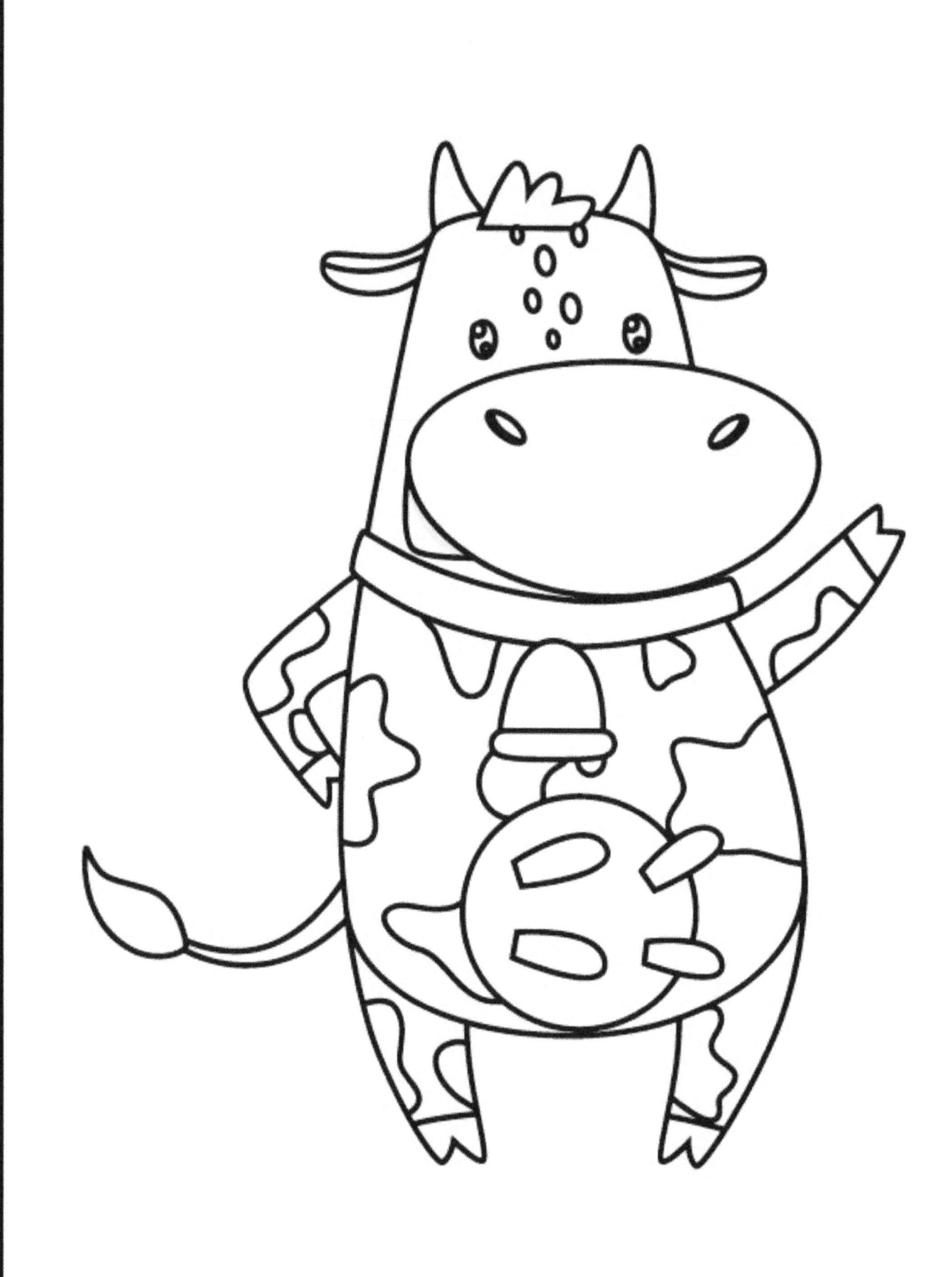

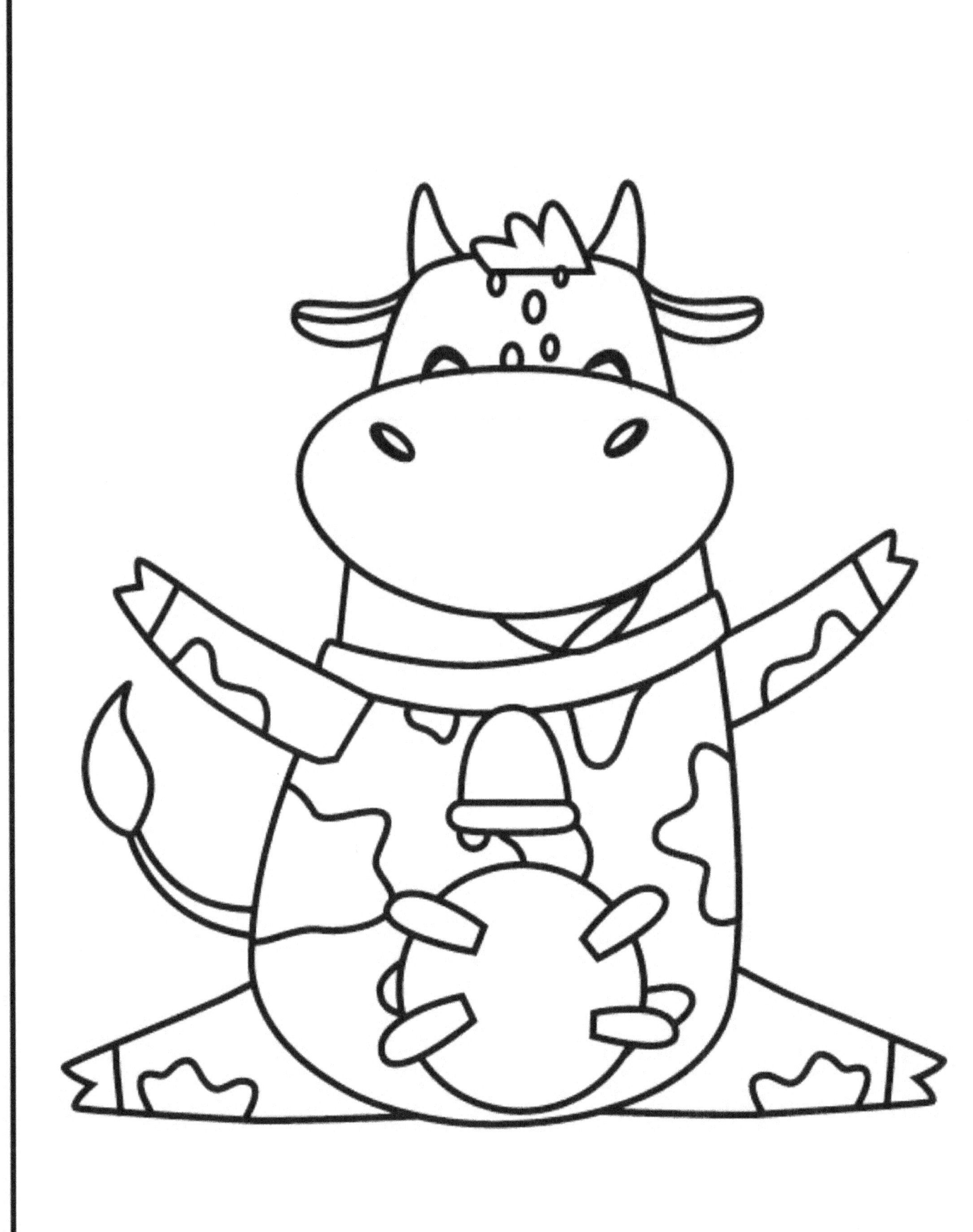

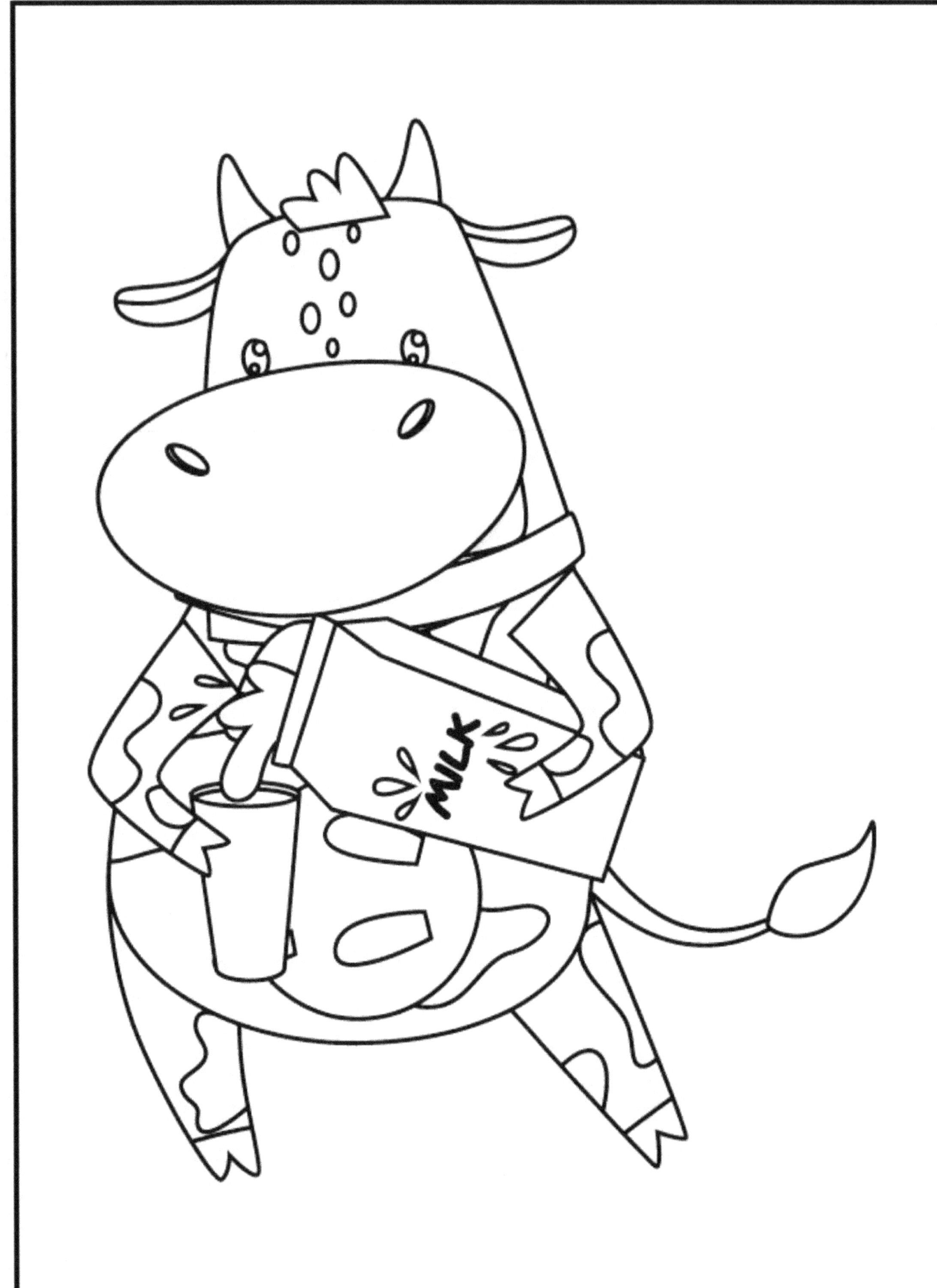
MILK

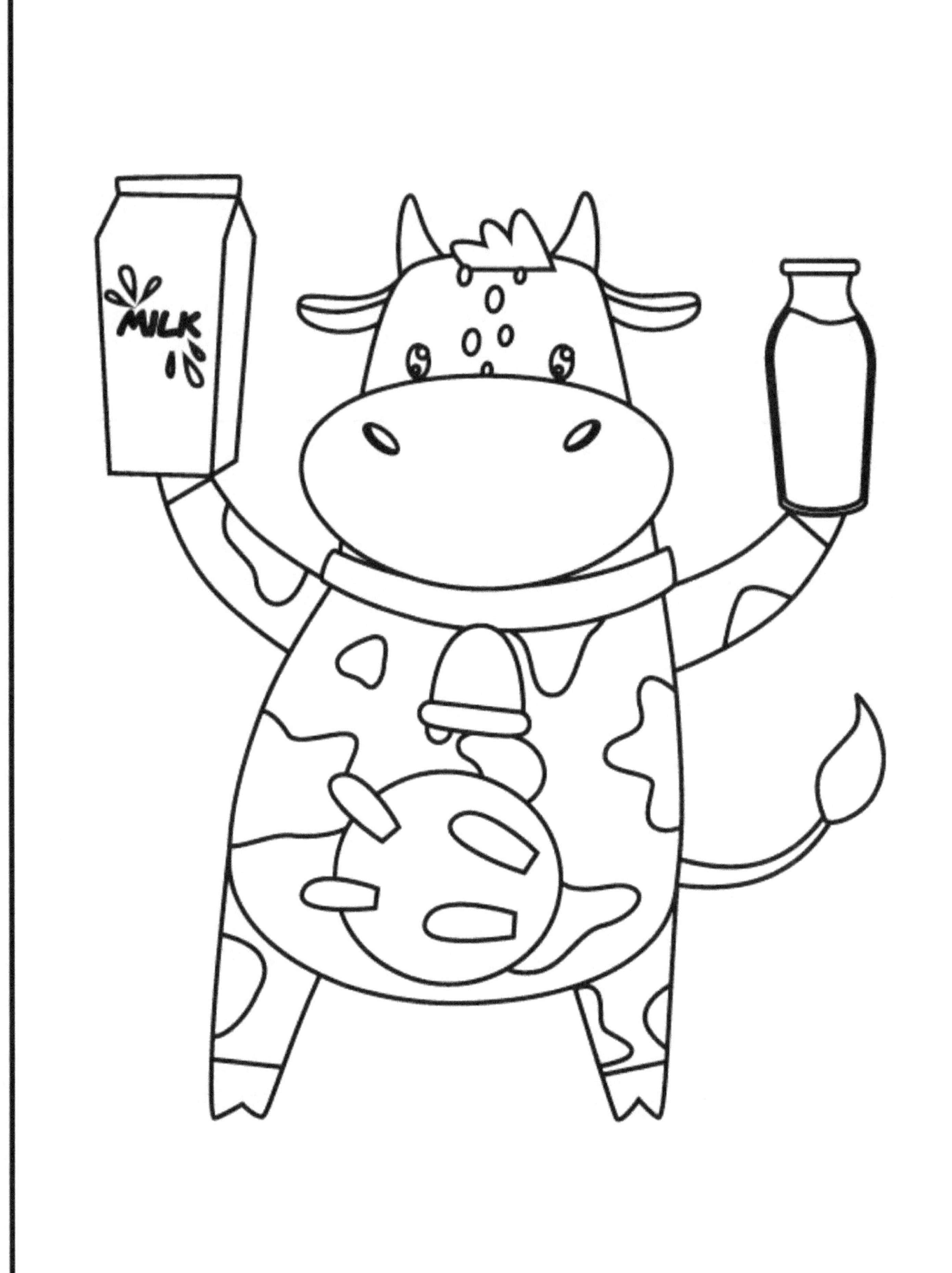
MILK

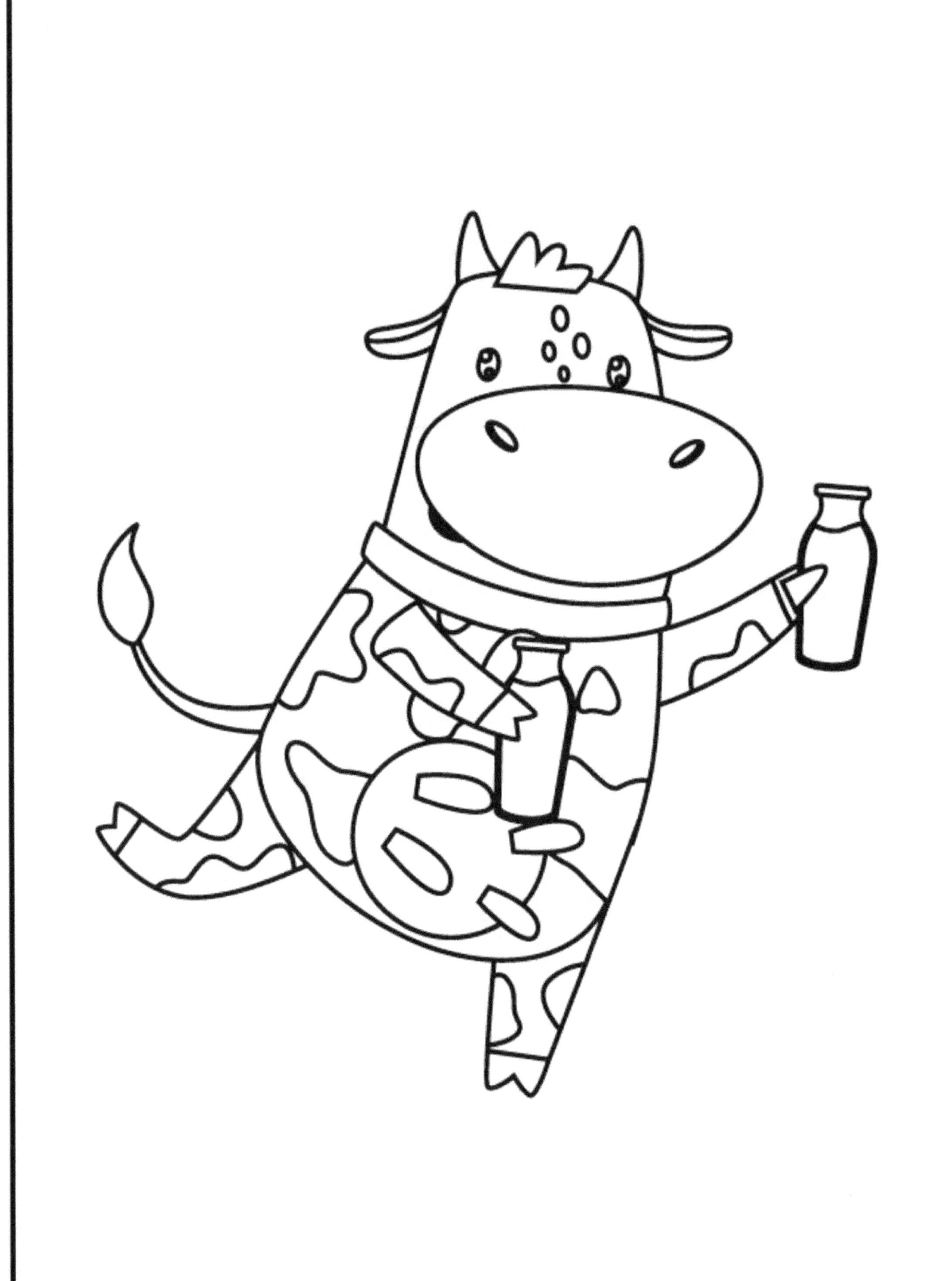

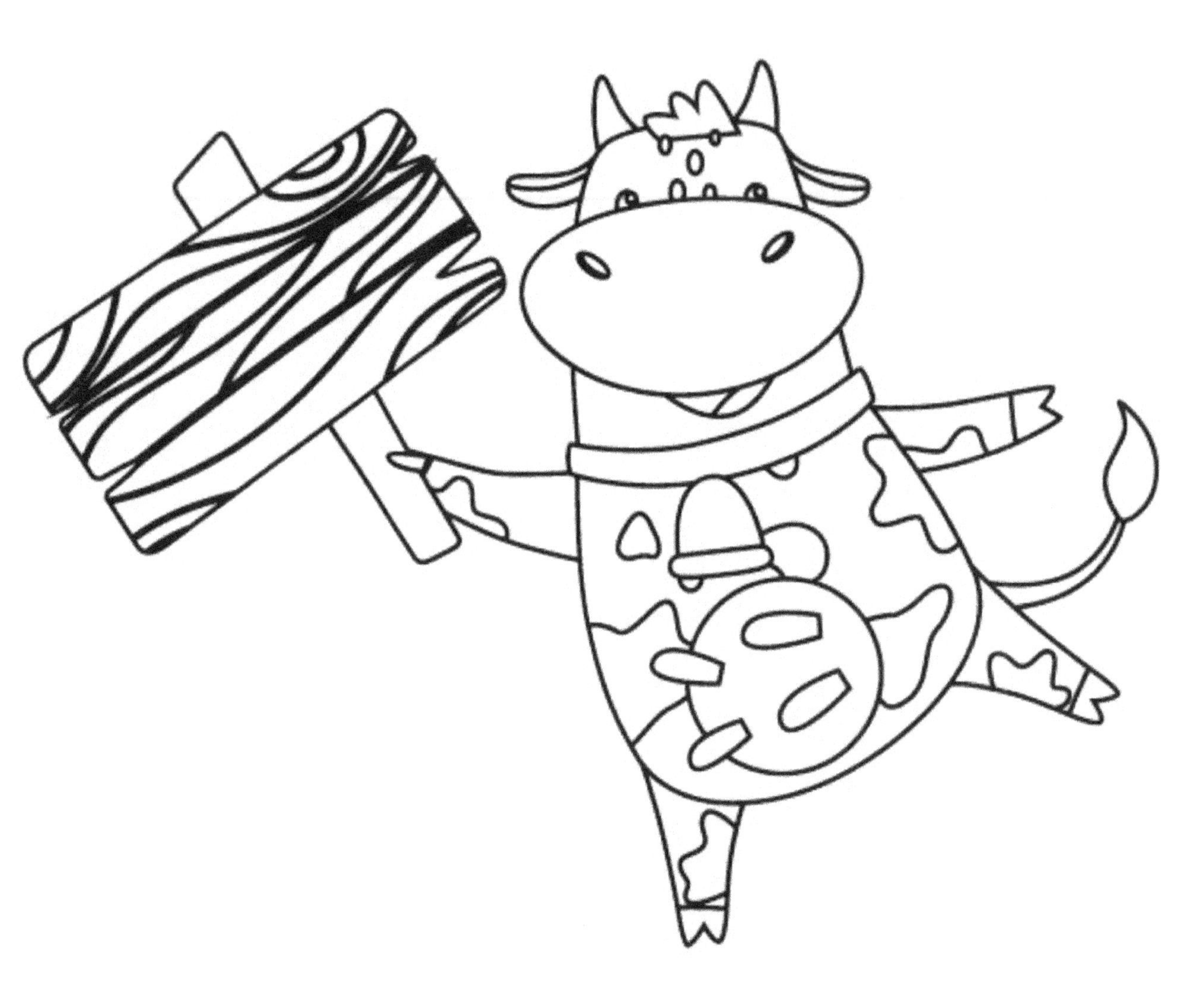

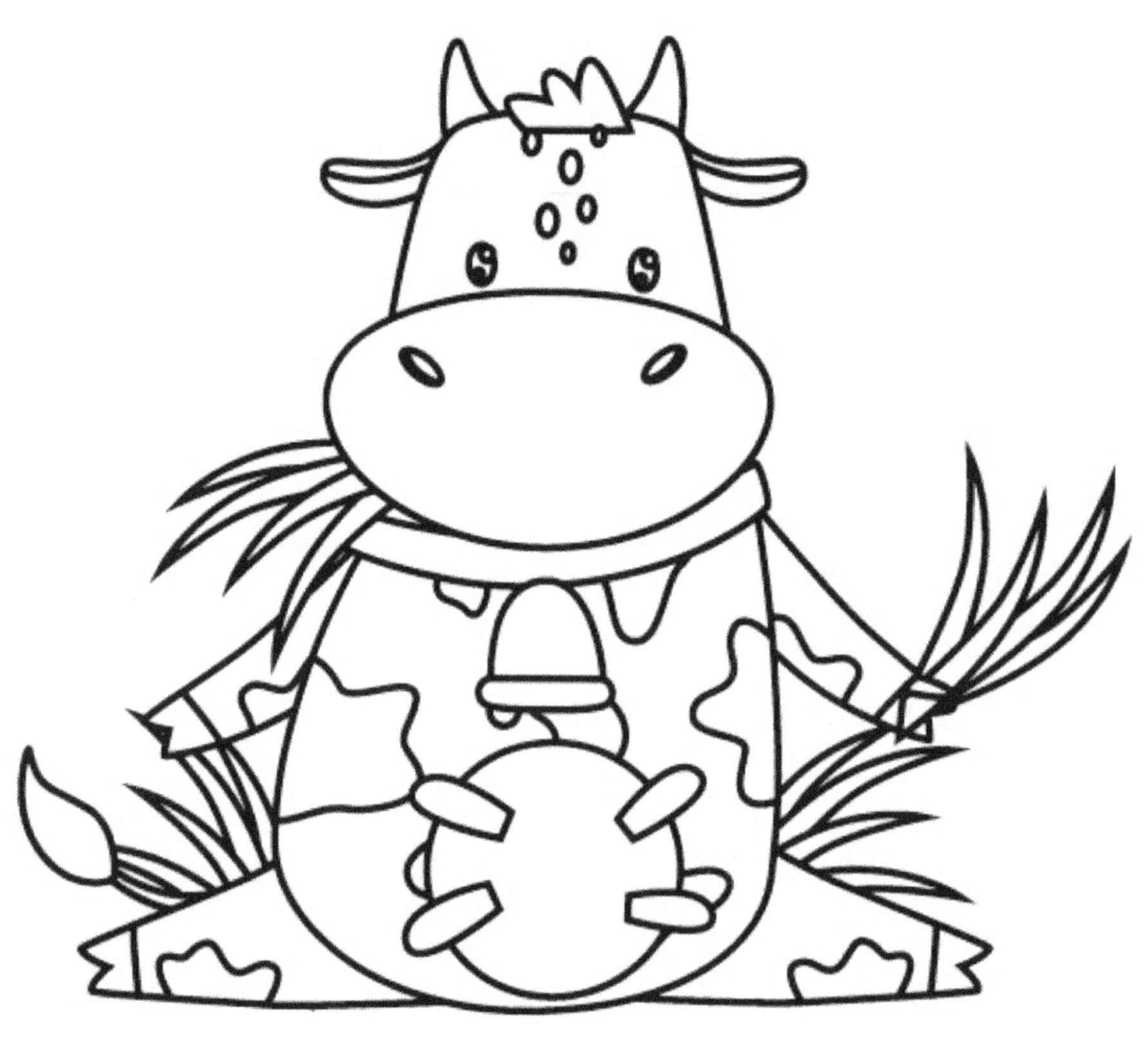

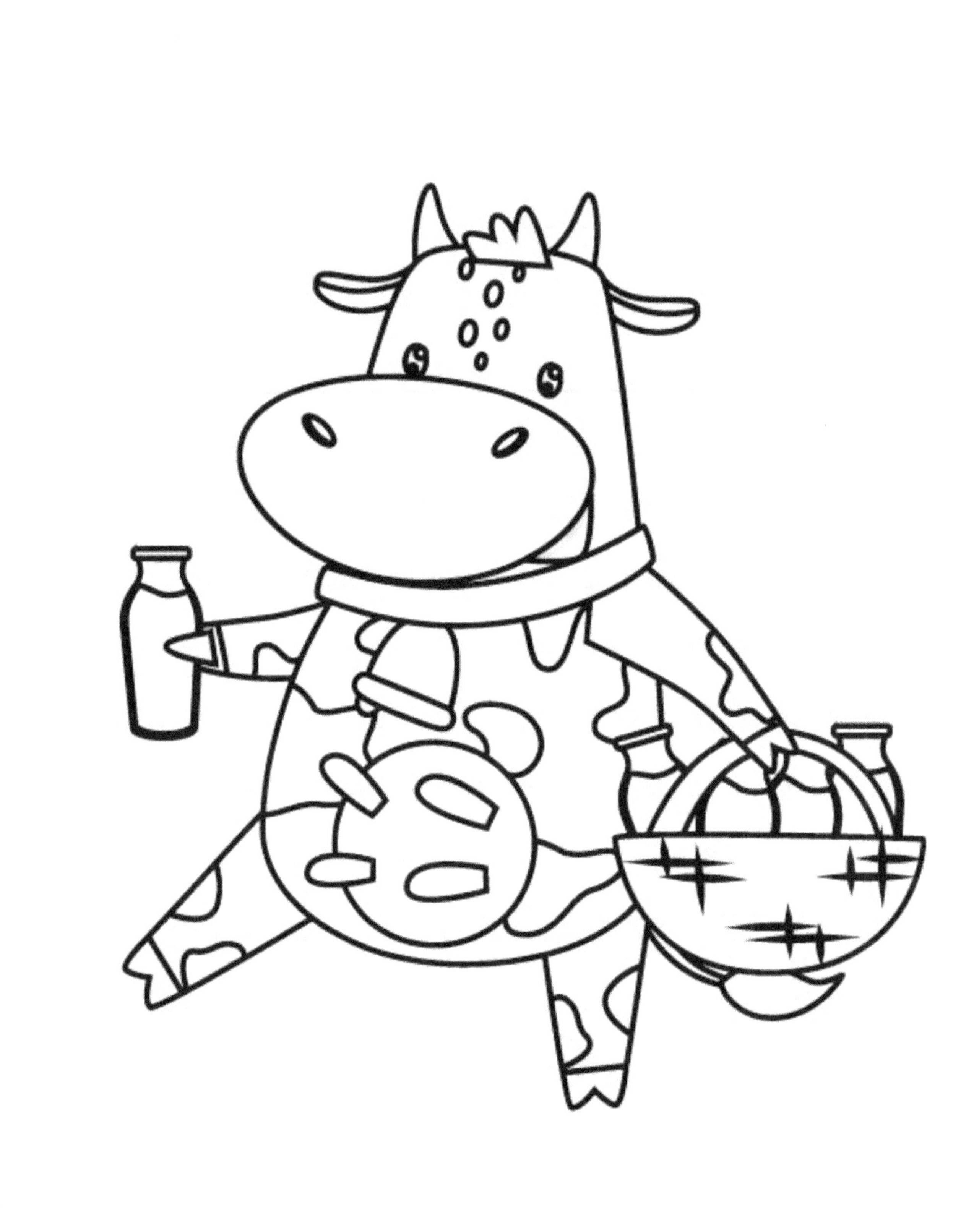

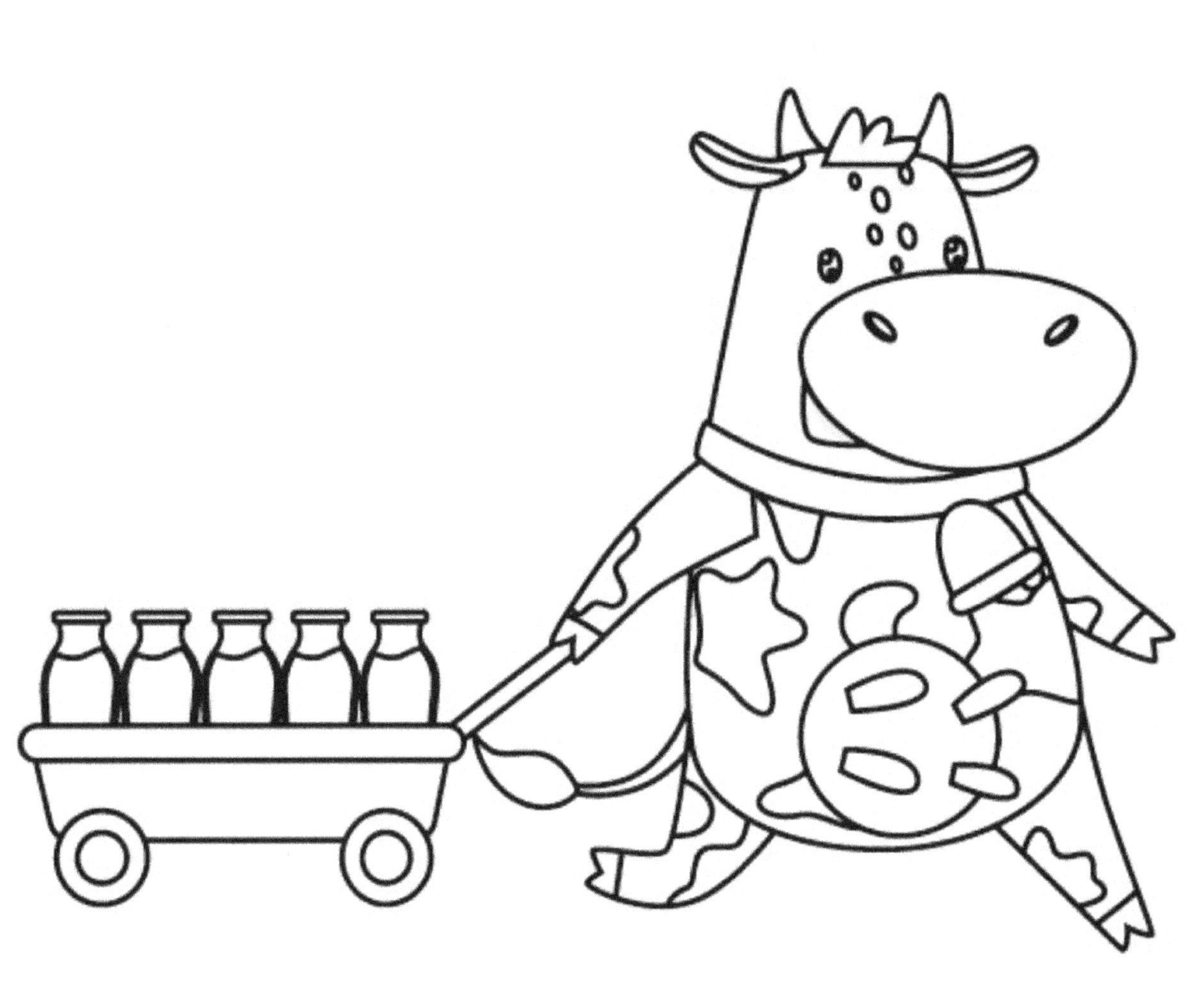

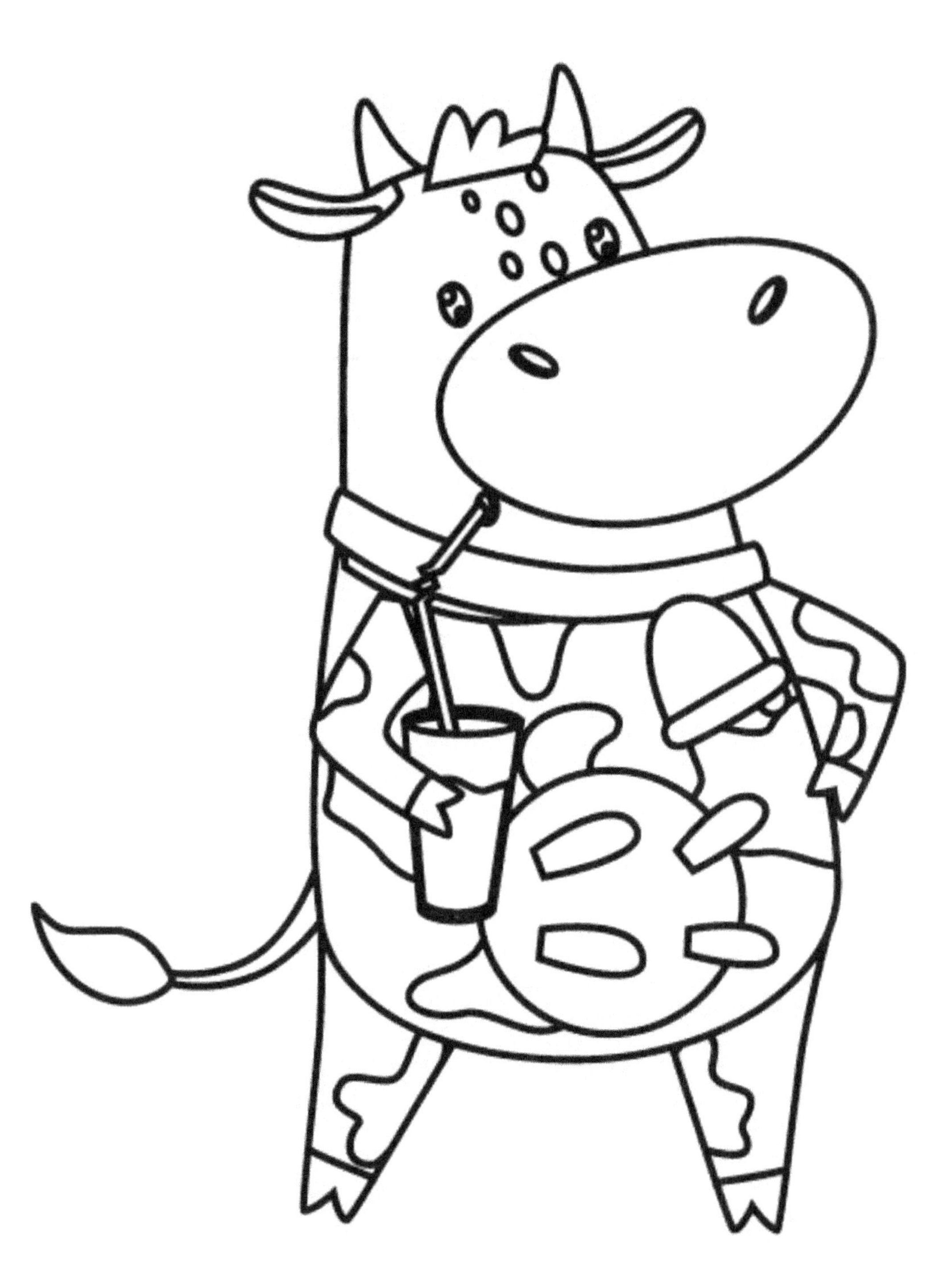

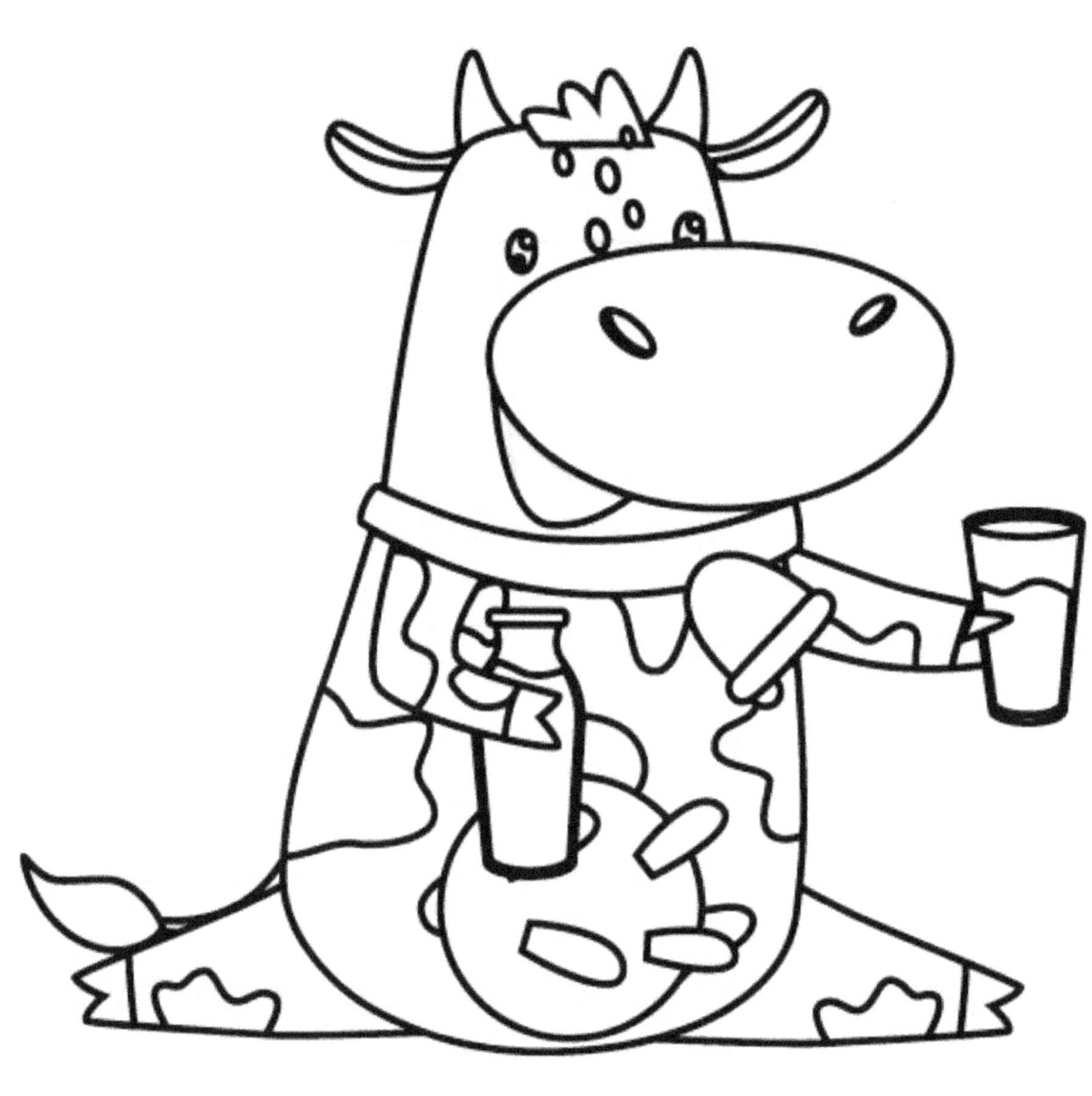

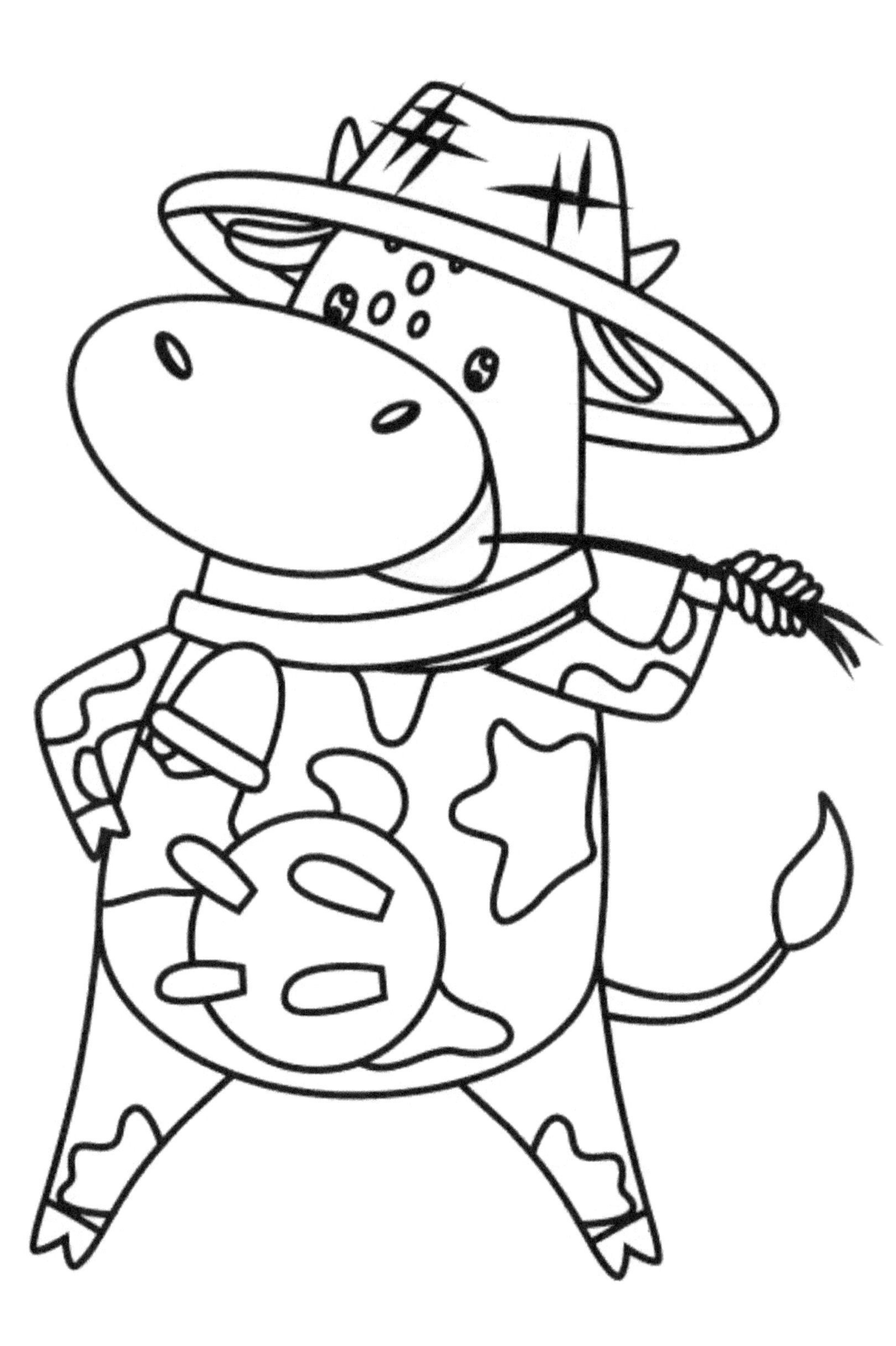

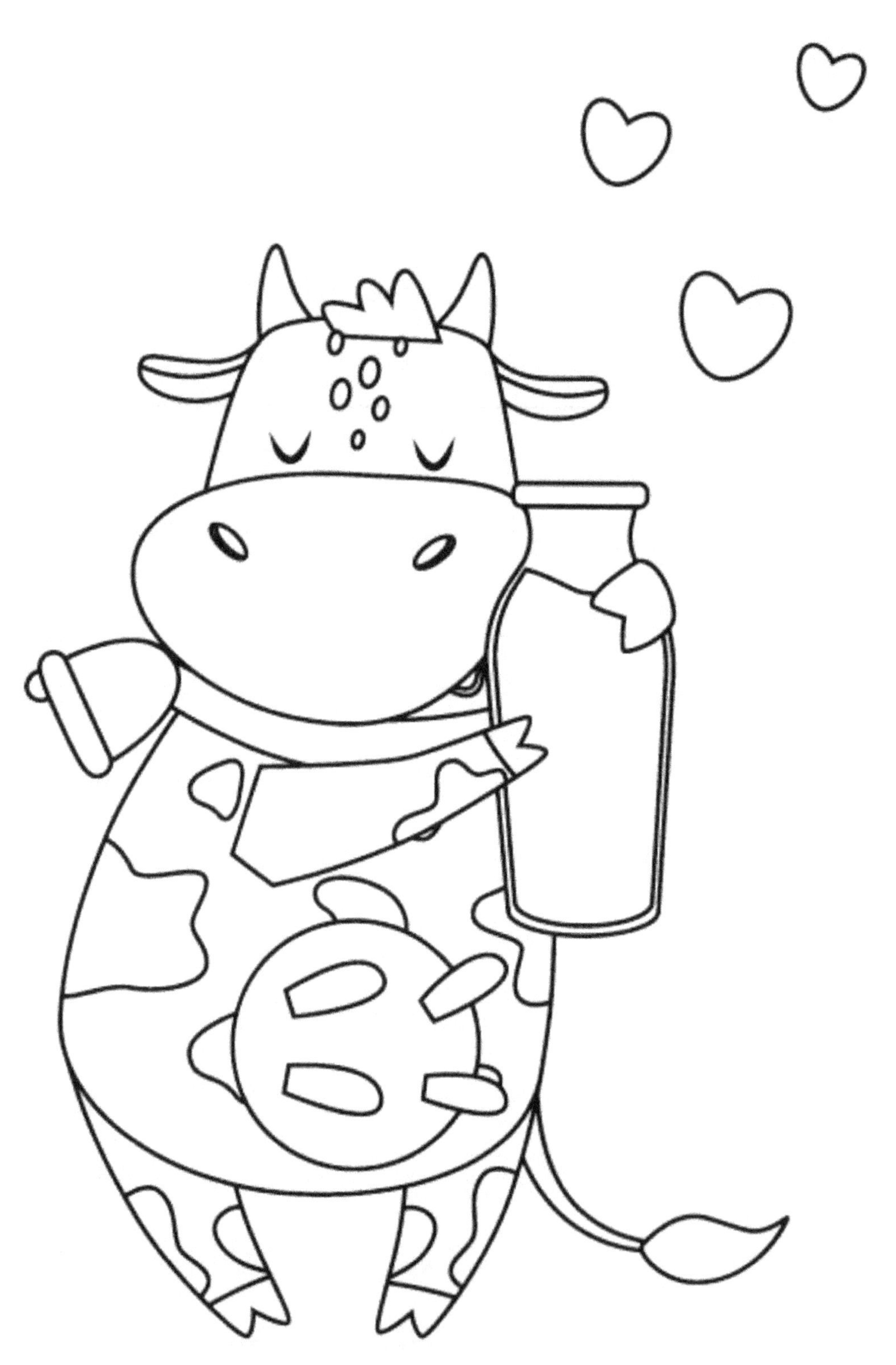

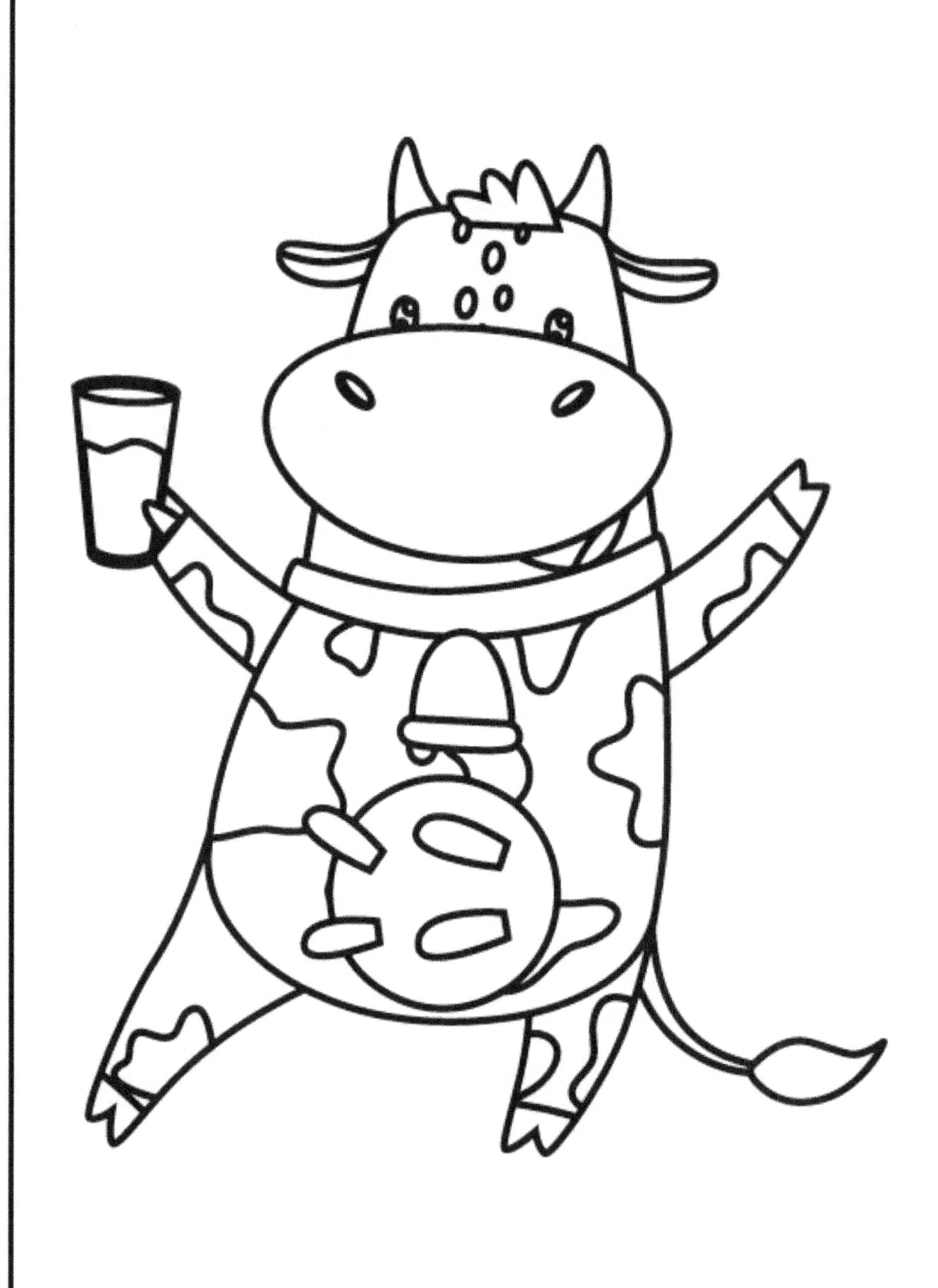

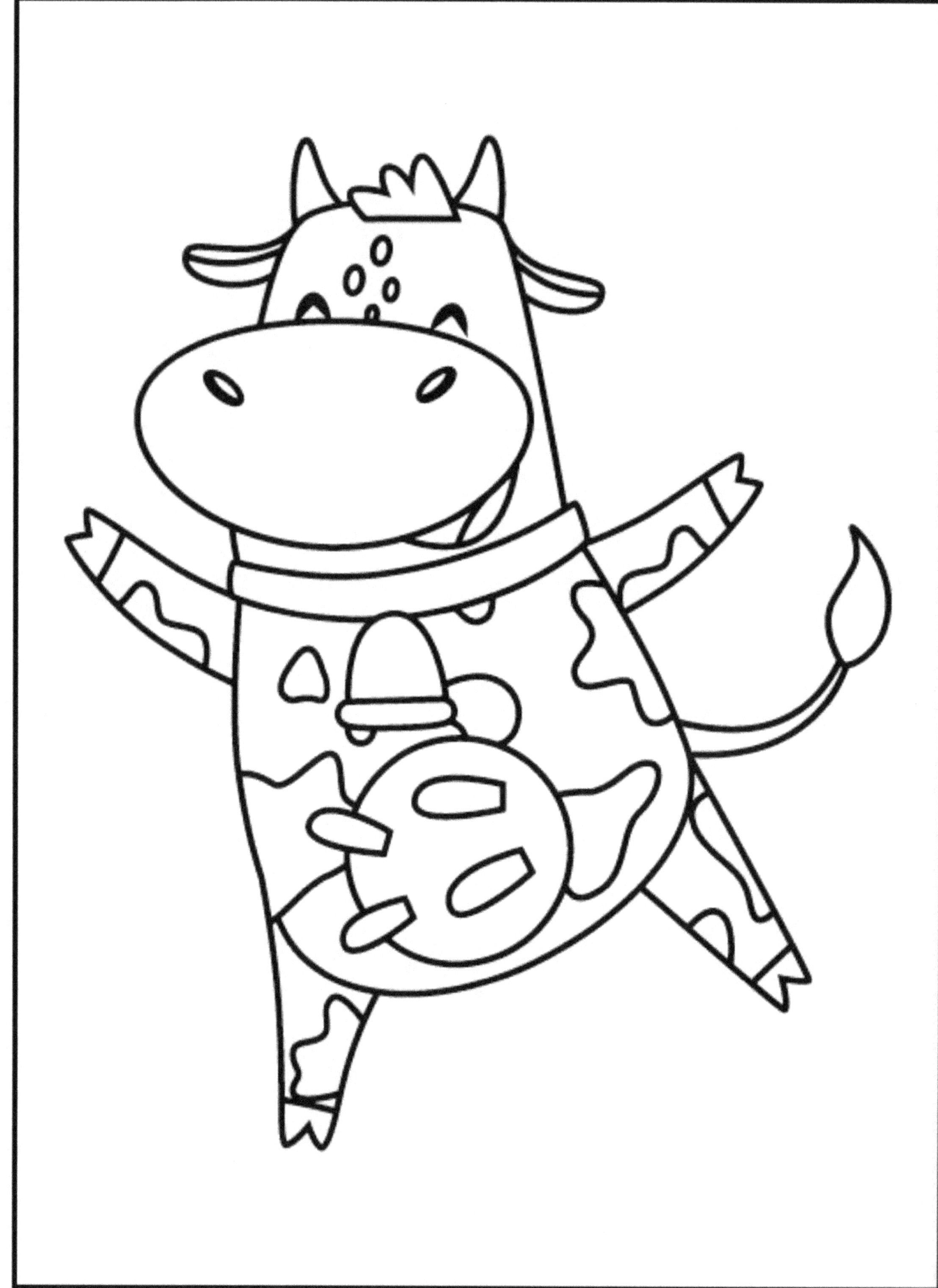

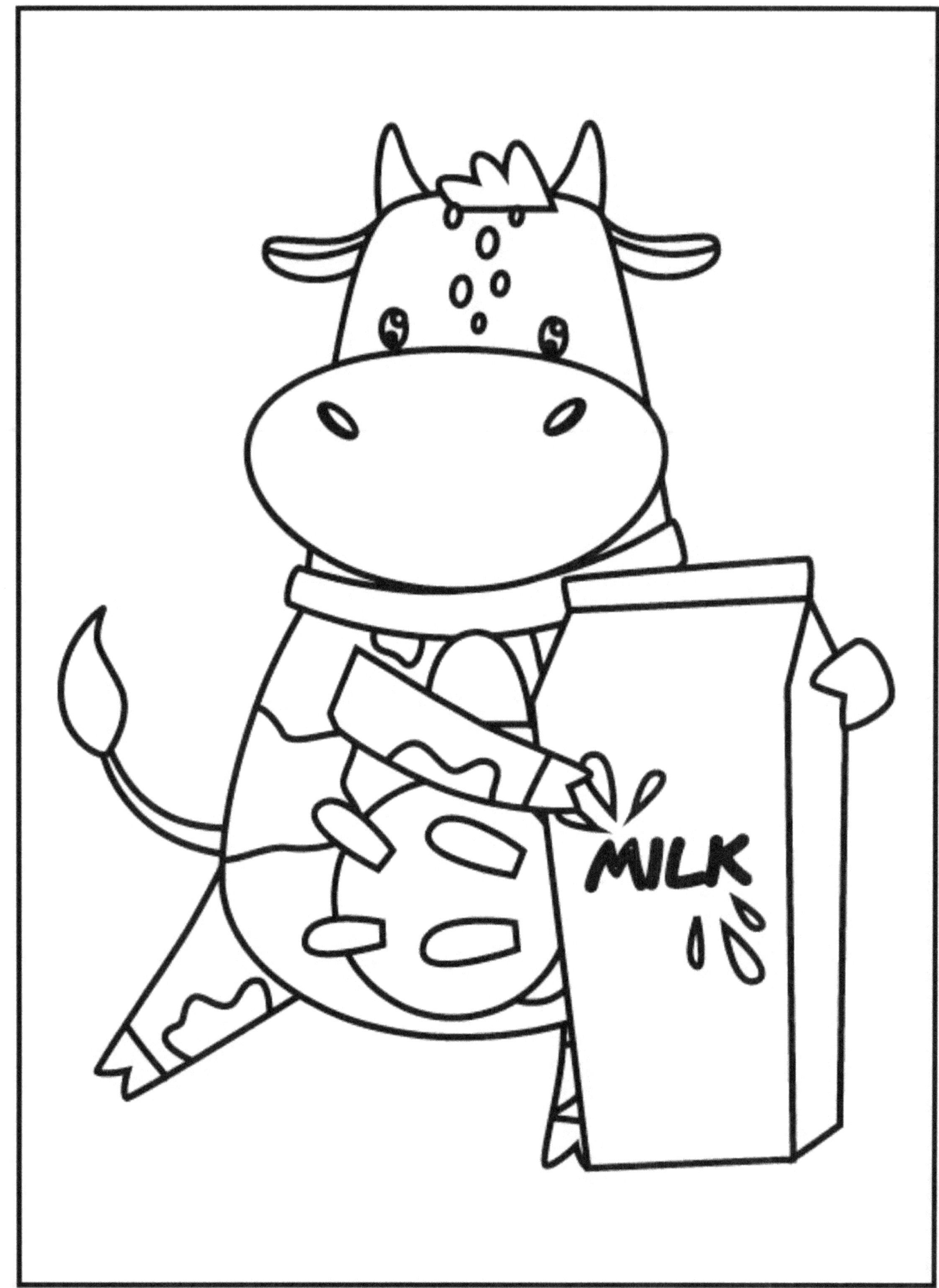

MILK

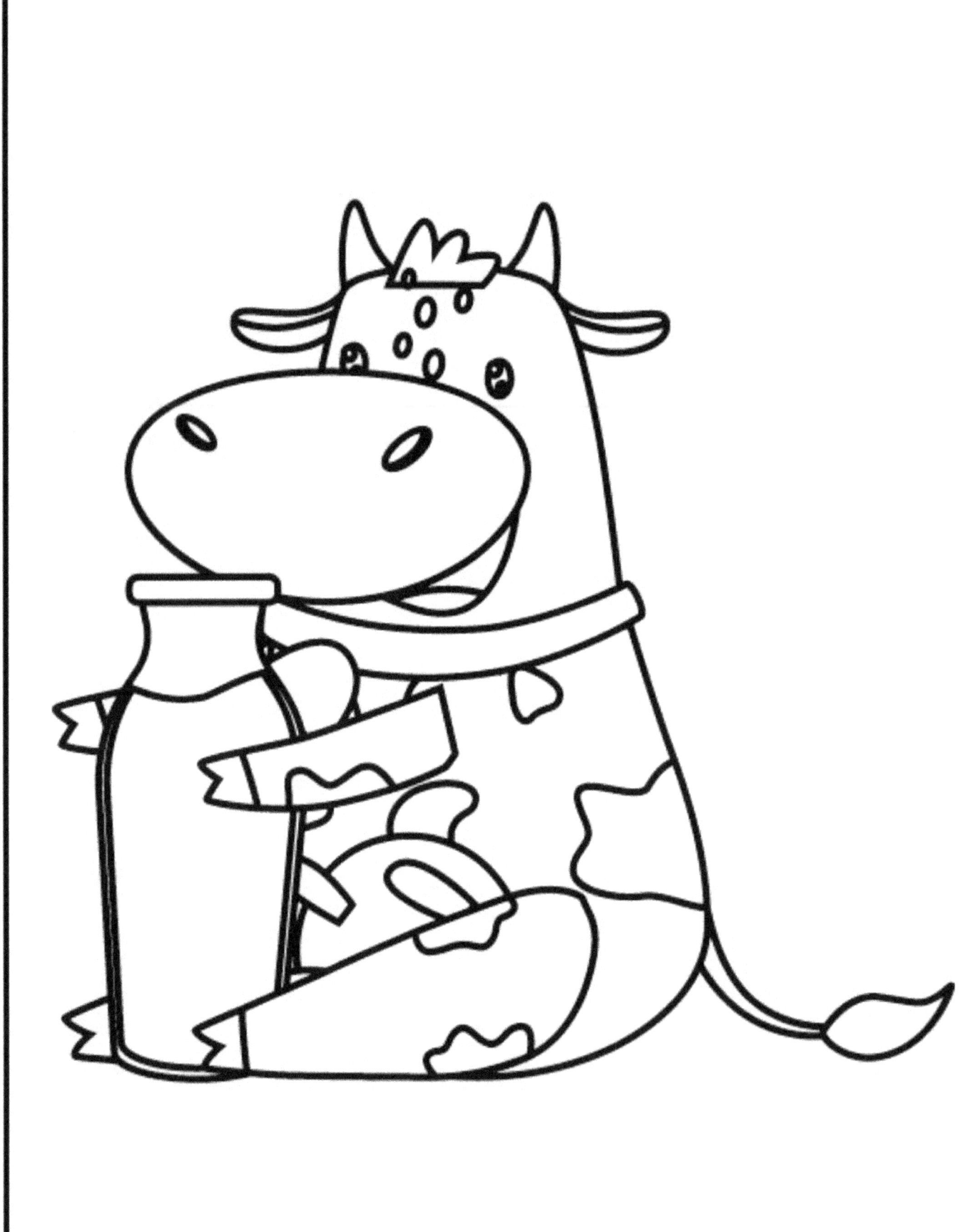

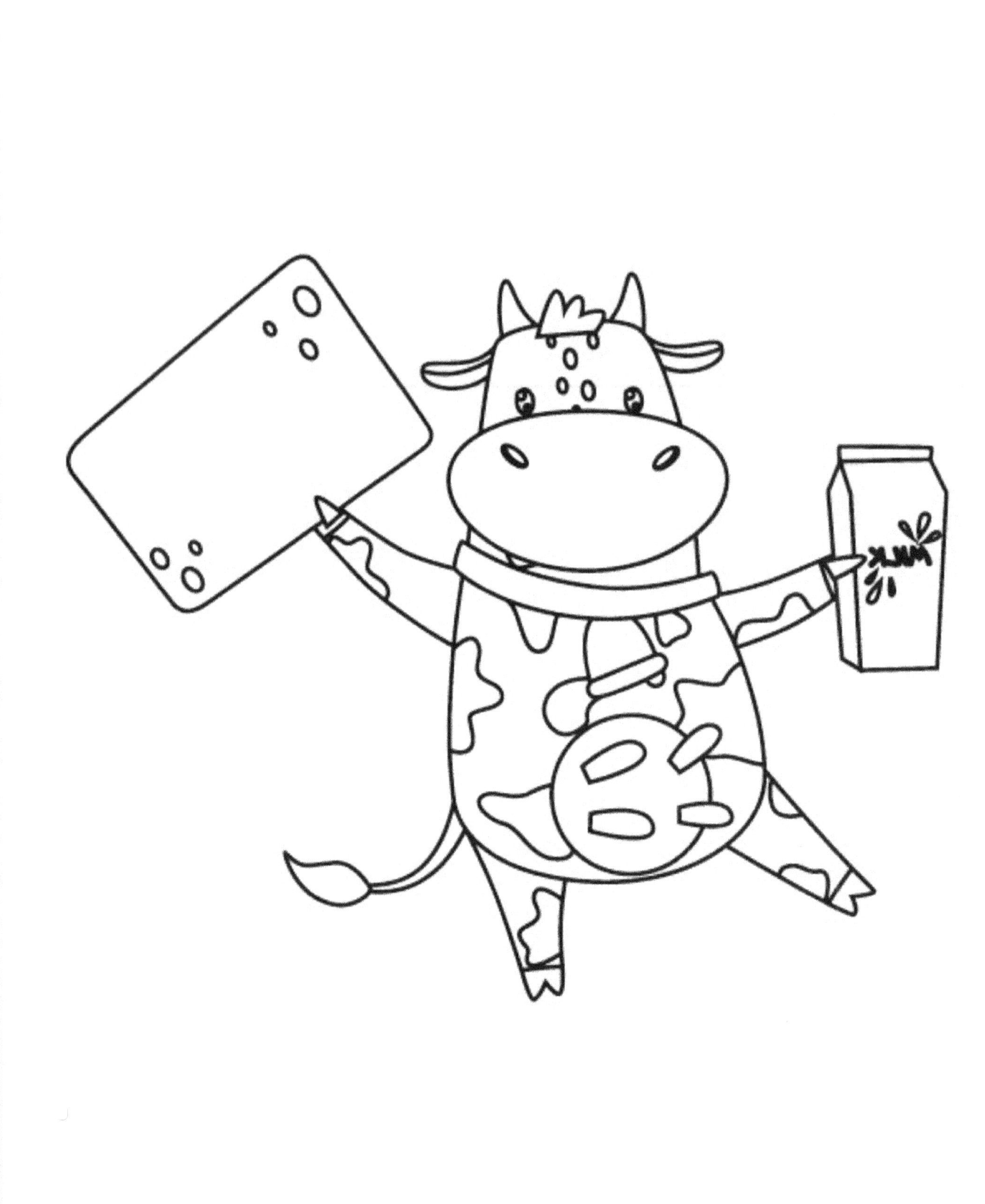
MILK

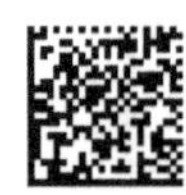

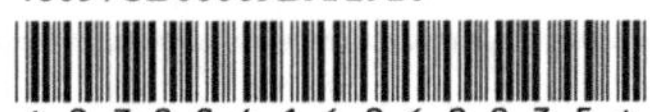